MW00634547

DENIAL

MELODY BEATTIE

HAZELDEN®

First published January, 1986.

Copyright © 1986, Hazelden Foundation.
All rights reserved. No portion of this publication
may be reproduced in any manner without the written
permission of the publisher.

ISBN: 0-89486-343-6

Printed in the United States of America.

FOREWORD

This pamphlet is one person's opinion — a person who regularly struggles with denial. But I have included quotes from experts to show what they think, too. I've also cited incidents and examples of how other people dealt with or solved a particular problem. The incidents are true, but I've used fictitious names to protect the anonymity of clients and friends.

I hope the booklet is helpful.

INTRODUCTION

Several years into her recovery program for alcoholism, Marjorie met and married a man. Seven chaotic years later, Marjorie realized that her husband was — and had been since they were married — an alcoholic, and that she was in trouble with her own compulsive, codependent behaviors. She was affected by alcoholism again, this time in a different way.

This awareness came suddenly, she said, as if someone had turned on a light switch inside her head. She spent the next several months depressed, angry, and fed up with herself. "I can't believe it took me seven years to see the truth. I knew all about alcoholism. How could I have denied it so long?" She asked. "What's wrong with me?"

You may have had a similar experience. You lived oblivious to a problem for a while, then had a light go on inside your head. Everything became clear — so clear you wondered how and why you couldn't see it before. Or you may know someone like Marjorie, who simply refuses to admit to or accept reality. She does not seem to see a thing that is right before her eyes. And no amount of arguing, cajoling, or insisting removes her blindfold. "People tried to tell me," Marjorie said. "They warned me, but I didn't hear them. What they said didn't register."

You may now be going through an experience like Marjorie's. You may feel uneasy, anxious, afraid, or downright desperate. Something isn't right, but you can't figure it out. You may have a vague idea what the problem involves; you may say it aloud sometimes. Others may be pointing it out to you in specific terms. But you don't hear yourself or them. You can't believe it!

Whether you or someone you know is affected by denial, the experience can be confusing and frustrating. You may care deeply about someone who seems hopelessly entangled in refusing reality. You may interpret his or her rejection of truth as stubbornness, stupidity, absurdity, and insanity. You may take it personally, as a rejection of your clear vision and

1

willingness to help. You may call it lying. You may wonder, like Marjorie did, what's wrong with him, her, or even yourself for not seeing reality clearly.

Although anyone may have some problems needing to be solved, there's nothing wrong with him or her for using denial. It's a coping mechanism people use to deal with pain and loss.

This booklet will go in search of an understanding and acceptance of denial as a legitimate tool and a valid stage in the grief, or acceptance, process. And what we will look at is not how to eliminate denial, but ways we can reduce our own and others' need to use it.

TOOL OR WEAPON?

Digging through the attic, Marcie, age seven, found a once-favorite ballet costume she had outgrown. In spite of her mother's protests, Marcie squeezed into the costume and wore it all day, oblivious to her absurd appearance.

Janet's oldest daughter, age fourteen, suddenly began doing poorly in school, acting withdrawn and defiant at home, and selecting friends who were doing the same. On several occasions, Janet found marijuana rolling papers in the child's bedroom. Twice, the child came home stumbling, slurring drunk. When a neighbor suggested to Janet that the daughter might be chemically dependent, Janet shrugged her off. "Not my daughter," she said.

Because of excessive drinking, Don had his driver's license revoked and lost his job. Upon threats of divorce from his wife, he reluctantly entered outpatient treatment for alcoholism. "I can't understand what everyone is fussing about," Don said to his counselor. "My drinking isn't that bad. I can control it. I'm not an alcoholic."

What is this fog that smothers people, choking off sensibility and blinding them to reality? What kind of change takes place, turning reasonable people into irrational beings? How can they stand there and say, "It just ain't so," when it is?

This fog is called denial. And it's not that they *won't* believe reality; they are involved in a process that is preventing them from believing it.

"In times of great stress, we shut down our awareness emotionally, sometimes intellectually, and occasionally physically," explained Claudia L. Jewett in *Helping Children Cope with Separation and Loss*. "A built-in mechanism operates to screen out devastating information and to prevent us from becoming overloaded. Psychologists tell us denial is a conscious or unconscious defense that all of us use to avoid, reduce, or prevent anxiety when we are threatened," Jewett continues. "We use it to shut out our awareness of things that would be too disturbing to know."[1]

When we use it, we short-circuit. We go numb. The person using denial may be lying, stubbornly refusing to admit the truth of a thing, performing mental gymnastics to make what is illogical appear logical, and defending it to you with the energy and vigor of an inflamed warrior protecting tribal territory. But this person is not just doing it to you. He's denying it to himself, too.

Noel Larson, a licensed consulting psychologist, defined denial at a Minnesota Corrections Conference on Sexual Assault. "Denial isn't lying," she said. "It's not letting yourself know what reality is."

Denial runs deep. We tell ourselves lies. When some awareness, some reality, threatens to hurt us, we trick ourselves into believing "it ain't so."

What are the jagged edges of life that provoke us into this temporary self-delusion? People may deny feelings, thoughts, events, changing conditions, situations, problems, illnesses, and even death itself. We deny the tangible and the intangible. People deny just about anything that can be denied — but what we usually deny is what we have lost, are losing, or suspect we're losing — something important to us.

The loss may be as minor as a five-dollar bill or as significant as our health. People lose all sorts of things that are important — love, loved ones, self-worth, faith in God, trust, dreams, jobs, health, money, possessions, independence, and even dependence. People may lose things that have become important to them but are difficult for others to see as losses — such as unhealthy relationships with people or chemicals.

All kinds of losses provoke all kinds of people to use denial. How hard and how long we deny varies. We may engage in a stunned second of disbelief. We may resist reality

---

[1] Jewett, Claudia L., Helping Children Cope With Separation and Loss (Harvard: The Harvard Common Press, 1982), pp. 23, 29.

for minutes, hours, days, or months. Or, we may spend years stumbling through a murky cloud.

Occasionally, denial is used to accomplish what some consider positive, heroic deeds. Oblivious to their pain, professional football players have — with broken bones — run the length of the field to score touchdowns. Sick mothers overlook their illnesses so they can care for young children. You may remember the story of the businessman who, after being injured in a plane crash, kept diving into the icy river to save fellow passengers until he finally died of injury, exposure, and exhaustion.

Denial is serious. When alcoholics deny their disease, they continue drinking themselves to death. Drug addicts deny they have a problem, and *get sicker*. Codependents of alcoholics and other drug addicts deny they have been affected by the disease and may continue to hurt themselves and others while using denial.

The problem here is painful and obvious. A person who denies reality is not admitting to, nor solving, the problem. Denial eliminates the possibility of change while it is being used. Whether what we're denying is a car problem, a character defect, or an alcohol problem, we're not going to fix it by saying it's not broken.

We are, at the same time, both sturdy and fragile beings. We have a great capacity to tolerate and endure change, pain, and loss. Remarkably, we can even grow from these things into more mature, sensitive, loving creatures. But at first, when loss comes to us, many of us need to say, "No. This cannot be true. This cannot be happening to me." Denial is a shock absorber for the soul.

It's a normal, natural, instinctive response to loss. It's a coping tool, some say God-given, that we use to deal with pain. We use it because we need to. We use it to deal with pain or problems by not dealing with them until we are ready and able to deal with them. And some of us may need a longer time and a little more help than others to "get ready."

"But isn't acceptance better?" you might ask. "Shouldn't a person be forced to see things realistically?" These are fair questions. Yes, acceptance is better. And confrontation and intervention, used properly and with care, are good therapeutic tools.

This is not to encourage anyone to choose or continue using denial. But we may want to keep in mind that, paradoxically, denial can be — and frequently is — the first step toward acceptance.

IT'S PART OF A PROCESS

People frequently misunderstand acceptance. "Just accept it," they say, as if acceptance was a single act, like closing the refrigerator door.

For me, acceptance does not come that easily. I don't immediately react with serenity to pain or problems. Now, I am usually grateful and content to be a recovering alcoholic and addict. I think it's fine to be both. In 1973, when I was first told I was an alcoholic and an addict and had to abstain from chemicals if I wanted to live, I did not respond to the news with ecstasy. I did not think it was fine. I went through a process to accept it. Bad news does not instantly become good news, or even neutral news. Most of us need to struggle with what we believe and how we feel before we can adjust to loss. We go through a process.

Elisabeth Kubler-Ross first observed and documented this five-stage process, the grief process, in her work with terminally ill hospital patients. She identified it as the way most dying people react to and reach acceptance of their impending death. In past years, many helping professionals have determined that people pass through these stages enroute to accepting all losses. Some treatment centers believe that this grief process is closely tied to acceptance and recovery from compulsive illnesses such as alcoholism, addiction, overeating, and gambling disorders because these illnesses produce so many losses.

We may find ourselves passing through these stages, at varying speeds and levels of emotion, when we miss an important phone call, get a displeasing haircut, lose our job, or get divorced. We may grieve whenever we experience change — even desired change — as any change means we've left something behind to make way for the new.

"No matter how trivial a loss might seem, the same process must be gone through each time, though the length and intensity of the experience will differ. It may take years to recover from a major loss. But the symptoms of grief and recovery can also be fully experienced in as little as ten seconds," writes Jewett.[2]

There is no rule for how long each stage will last; there is no rule for how long the entire process takes. That will depend on the nature of the loss, how equipped we are to deal with loss, how we have dealt with other losses, and God's timing. People will take as long as they need to work through it. Growing people is more complicated than growing flowers or vegetables.

Although five distinct stages can be outlined on paper, our passage through them may not be as distinct. The stages may overlap; we may experience more than one stage at one time. We may return to previous stages. We may be at different stages of the process for two or more losses simultaneously. We may whip through it three times in the same day.

Sometimes, in the case of ongoing losses, we may never reach permanent acceptance. This is true when the loss continues to affect our day-to-day living. Parents of a handicapped child may experience stages of the grief process all of their lives — particularly as new implications of the child's handicap develop. Because alcoholism is a lifelong, incurable disease, and because it's cunning and baffling, alcoholics may

---

[2] Ibid.

never safely assume they have reached final acceptance of their illness. They are at great risk for reverting to denial — one reason it's important for alcoholics to treat their illness by attending A.A. meetings. Ongoing acceptance may require ongoing attention.

This acceptance process is a spiritual one. It is a going-through and a letting-go experience. I have heard people call it the grief, mourning, forgiveness, and the healing process. Esther Olson, counselor and author, gave my favorite description. "It's the way God works with us," she said.

Following is a discussion of each stage.

Denial

Denial is the first reaction to loss. In the same way that severe physical pain or injury may cause our bodies to go into shock, emotional and mental pain can cause a similar reaction in our feelings, intellect, and sometimes our bodies. We go numb, short circuit. Some therapists call this a "block." Most professionals agree it is usually not a complete block. Part of us knows or suspects the truth. We just aren't ready or able to deal with it yet.

Again, there is no rule for how long denial lasts. Each person and each situation is unique. People will deny until they feel safe enough to cope with the loss another way.

Once a person overcomes denial, however, it is still not time to bask in acceptance. Watch out. Hell knows no fury like one who has moved into the next stage.

Anger

This stage is characterized by blame, envy, resentment, and sometimes rage. Our anger may be specific and pointed, or it may be general, cast randomly into our environment. It may be irrational or rational, justified or unjustified, sensible or senseless. We may kick the cat and holler at the kids, but not really be mad at either. We're angry about our loss. We may blame others and ourselves for the spot we now find ourselves in. We may find ourselves envying those who have what we have lost. "Why can he have a cocktail before dinner and not end up smashed and senseless by midnight?" We may harangue and carry on endlessly, harbor and spew bad feelings, or explode in a deep and violent unleashing. This rage can sometimes be dangerous, both to the person feeling it and the person who is the object of it.

We switch, in this stage, from "Not me!" to "Why me?" "It's your fault," and "It's not fair." We're mad. Usually underneath the anger lurk fear, guilt, and shame.

Just as we needed to deny, we now need to be angry. "It's okay to go through this stage," says Olson. "Anger will be a propellant if not dealt with. But we need to deal with our anger appropriately."

Bargaining

After venting our fury, we may try to make a bargain that will prevent or postpone the loss. These negotiations may be made with God or vaguely with life. This stage is usually characterized by *if . . . , then . . .* statements which measure what we give against what we get, according to Olson. Sometimes our bargains are constructive, realistic, and do the job. "If we get help for our marriage, then we won't have to get divorced." "If I get help for my drinking problem, then I won't have to die."

Usually, however, our bargains are not this realistic. The alcoholic may strike up a bargain to drink only beer, or to drink on only one weekend a month. "I kept thinking, 'If I really clean the house well this time, then he won't get angry and drink,' " said the spouse of one alcoholic. In these cases, when we can no longer postpone the inevitable, we experience it.

Depression

We now move into a period of sadness. Ever since we first said, "This cannot be true," we have been swept toward this moment. It is perhaps the essence of grief — mourning at its fullest. It is the peak of the acceptance process and it is emotional pain at its purest. We grieve over what we have lost, and over what we will lose in the future. This is the time to cry.

This sadness may last hours, days, weeks, or months. "When we humbly surrender, this process begins," says Olson. "This depression will disappear only when the process has been worked out."

Acceptance

When we no longer need to block, be angry, or make deals, and when we have worked through our sadness, we will have arrived at that stage called acceptance.

"It is not a resigned and hopeless 'giving up,' a sense of 'what's the use?' or 'I just cannot fight it any longer,' though we hear such statements too," writes Kubler-Ross in *On Death and Dying*. "They also indicate the beginning of the end of the struggle, but the latter are not indications of acceptance. Acceptance should not be mistaken for a happy stage. It is almost void of feelings. It is as if the pain had gone, the struggle is over. . . ."[3]

We are at peace with what is, and freely admit our power-lessness over alcohol or the alcoholic. God has granted us the serenity to accept that which we could not change.

Following acceptance, we grow. This implies we have not merely endured the experience, we have been changed or improved by it. In some way, we consider ourselves enriched. If we cannot see how it has benefited us, then we at least have a bit of trust that it has been right, that all is well, and that someday we may understand the purpose.

We can accept loss and grow, but the journey is not easy, nor is it particularly comfortable. It can be awkward and

---

[3] Kubler-Ross, Elisabeth, *On Death and Dying* (NY: Macmillan Publishing Co., 1969), pp. 99-100.

often seems like it will shake us apart. The moment it begins, we may feel shock and panic. During it, we may feel confused, vulnerable, lonely, and isolated. We may experience a sense of loss of control. We need to rely on the grace of a Higher Power; we need to cling to hope. In all stages except denial, hope is a lifeline.

It is important to understand and make a commitment to this process. It's valid, beneficial, and necessary for acceptance.[4]

Going through this process is also important to our health. Mourning is not new to this decade or century. Jesus mentioned it in the beatitudes: "Blessed are they that mourn, for they shall be comforted."[5] In a search to understand what "blessed" meant, Donald L. Anderson, a minister and psychologist, rephrases that verse in *Better Than Blessed.* "Healthy are those who mourn," he writes. "Only very recently have we begun to realize that to deny grief is to deny a natural human function and that such denial sometimes produces dire consequences," he continues. "Grief, like any genuine emotion, is accompanied by certain physical changes and the release of a form of psychic energy. If that energy is not expended in the normal process of grieving, it becomes destructive within the person. . . . Even physical illness can be a penalty for unresolved grief. . . . Any event, any awareness that contains a sense of loss for you can, and should, be mourned. This doesn't mean a life of incessant sadness. It means being willing to admit to an honest feeling rather than always having to laugh off the pain. It's not only permissible to admit the sadness that accompanies any loss — it's the healthy option."[6]

---

[4] Ibid, p. 78.

[5] New Testament, King James Version, Matthew 5:4

[6] Anderson, Donald L., Ph.D., *Better Than Blessed,* (Wheaton, Ill: Tyndale House Publishers, 1981), p. 18

And it helps to understand grief. People who hurt are going through it. We need to allow ourselves, and others, the freedom to struggle through, feel, and talk about it — if they wish.

Remember Marjorie in the first section of this pamphlet? She is the recovering alcoholic who spent seven years denying her husband was an alcoholic. After she stopped denying, she went through an intense period of anger and depression. During this time she became frightened and confused. "I think I'm going crazy," she confided. "I haven't been this depressed since my own treatment for alcoholism."

When Marjorie understood she was not going crazy, but experiencing grief, she felt better. She still felt sad, but she understood why. It was okay. She was okay.

Understanding the process won't eliminate our need to go through it, but it will help us relax, be less fearful, and work with it, instead of against it. And we can be of greater help to others.

Now that we've examined denial's place in the scheme of acceptance, let's discuss what denial looks like, both from the outside and the inside.

LOOKS LIKE/FEELS LIKE/SOUNDS LIKE

How can we recognize when we are using denial? Is it as easy as discovering an elephant sitting in the middle of our house?

It would be convenient if recognizing denial were that simple. What we deny is a problem, loss, or feeling in the midst of our lives. It's what we walk around, dodge, and run away from. In spite of our efforts, it's also what we keep bumping into.

Despite ongoing brushes with the object of our denial, it may be difficult to recognize that we or someone else is immersed in it. We may be so close to a situation that we don't see it clearly. We may be so provoked with someone's outrageous behavior that we aren't thinking clearly. We may be so busy responding to the symptoms — the stubborness, the absurdity, or the lying — that we don't take time to identify the problem. We don't look at the fog — we focus on the person stumbling around in it.

We may also get caught in the fog. We may have a need to deny whatever it is another person is denying. For purely personal reasons, we may need our spouses to not be alcoholic or our children to not be in trouble. So when they say "it just ain't so," we may be eager to agree.

Another problem is that recognizing when we are using denial is like realizing we're asleep. We realize when it's over that we've been doing it, but we don't think much about it while we're doing it.

In spite of the difficulty in recognizing denial, we can learn to become sensitive to its presence. Each person is unique; each denial system will be unique. But experts have identified certain common emotional, mental, and behavioral patterns.

Some cues may indicate a person is using denial. A person may use more than one at the same time, or he may switch back and forth as the occasion demands. A hearty denier (yes, alcoholics, I'm referring to us) may use many of the systems at once in grand, dazzling orchestration.

Before you grab your pencil and rip out the following pages to use as a checklist for inspecting your family and neighbors, I suggest you begin by studying yourself. And when you've finished with you, remember to use your information not to judge others, but to behave in more helpful and healthy ways toward them.

Don't fret about whether you're pinpointing all the denial systems in your life. I have been told by A.A. members that we don't need to be aware of all our problems and issues at once. If we are working our program and living as we should, we will become aware of the things we need to work on when it's time. We'll face our problems when we're supposed to face them.

Caution: The presence of any of the following traits is never certain proof of denial.

Looks like. . .

The four main ways people deny, according to Jewett,[7] are by:

1. *Refusing to believe reality.* This is characterized by statements like, "I don't believe it," "It can't be true," and "This couldn't happen to me." We then proceed to conduct ourselves as though the event, problem, or loss doesn't exist. Sometimes, we may act as though we acknowledge the problem, but we're really only adapting under pressure. Deep inside we're whispering, "No. Not me."

2. *Denying or minimizing the importance of the loss.* Here, we are saying whatever happened is "no big deal." We admit to the reality of a thing, but insist it is not as serious as others think; we may even accuse them of overreacting. We conduct ourselves as though we don't consider the problem important.

3. *Denying any feelings about the loss.* This is emotional repression. "It happened — it's happening — but I don't care," we tell ourselves and others. We may act and look like we don't care, appearing emotionally flat.

4. *Mental avoidance.* We avoid things mentally in several ways. We may sleep excessively to escape (actually feeling *that* tired). We may become hyperactive — darting from activity to activity, not slowing until we collapse at night. We may become driven by compulsions or obsessions. We may lose ourselves under the headphones, in front of the television, or in reading materials. We might look like we're running, dodging, avoiding, and escaping. We are!

People who are avoiding reality will also go to great lengths to escape situations that confront their denial system. They

---

[7] Jewett, Claudia L., *Helping Children Cope With Separation and Loss* (Harvard: The Harvard Common Press, 1982), p. 29.

are having enough difficulty repressing the truth — they don't need to place themselves in a spot that will make it more difficult. Instead, they will seek out situations that reinforce their denial. Friends, social events, sometimes even career choices, will be made on this basis. Alcoholics and drug addicts have been known to structure their entire lives in a manner that supports their denial.

Feels like. . .

1. A person using denial may feel desperate, alone, confused, uneasy, anxious, driven, frightened, guilty, vulnerable, or out of control.

2. Conversely, a person may feel nothing; emotions are flat, bland, shut down, cold, or repressed.

3. Responses to situations may be inappropriate: giddiness when sadness would fit the occasion, unhappiness or anger when elation would be appropriate. Sometimes we are amazed at how well a person responds to a tragedy. "He's not crying, not falling apart. Could we handle things so efficiently?" we wonder. Probably, if denial had set in.

4. Besides feeling tired because of the great sleep escape, the denier may feel unusually tired because denial, and the entire grieving process, is fatiguing. "Keeping reality from emerging to consciousness is like trying to hold a basketball under water," writes Anderson. "You can do it — but it takes concentration and energy."[8]

5. When in denial, we often feel defensive about whatever we are denying. Others may sense this, whether or not it's said aloud, and think, "I'd better not talk about this, or there'll be a scene." So the problem cannot be discussed.

6. A feeling of detachment or disconnection from one's self is common in denial. We may notice we feel out of touch

---

[8]Anderson, Donald L., Ph.D., *Better Than Blessed* (Wheaton, Ill: Tyndale House Publishers, Inc., 1981), p. 31

with ourselves and our ability to think and feel. Sometimes, in traumatic incidents, we may actually have a sense of being outside ourselves, watching. "It was as if the experience didn't happen to me. I was there, watching another person go through it — only that person was me," one person reported after a severe crisis. We may sense this disconnection and lack of closeness in someone who is using denial. It may seem the person has gone away and cannot make contact.

7. Extended denial may cause a person to feel and actually become sick, mentally or physically. A person may have headaches, stomach aches, back problems, and sexual dysfunctions. A person using denial may be less resistant to all illnesses, and may get sick more frequently than usual.

Sounds like. . .

People using denial may tell themselves and others that:

1. It's not that bad, that much, or that often (minimization).
2. It's not important.
3. It's not so. Couldn't be.
4. I don't care.
5. I'm too busy or tired to think about it, much less discuss it.
6. It'll all be better in the morning.
7. I'm not as bad as Harvey. My situation is not as bad as Harvey's (comparison).
8. It was really exciting and fun — which it wasn't (euphoric recall).
9. I did it, but. . .(or because. . .). It was sensible (rationalization).
10. I did it, but. . . (or because. . .). It was the right thing to do (justification).
11. I don't have that problem, but an awful lot of people around me do (projection).
12. I couldn't be that way because I'm forever acting the opposite (compensation).

13. Many other creative combinations of the above.

This list is not meant to be complete, but only to give you an idea of the communication that accompanies denial. The rationale sounds good, almost logical (if we don't listen too closely), and convincing. After all, they're convincing themselves. We may find ourselves nodding our heads in agreement while the denier is talking, then wondering what just happened. We've been bamboozled, but we're not sure how or why.

GENTLE: HUMAN BEINGS IN PROCESS

The first time I watched a professional work with a denying person, I thought I was watching magic. I also thought he was doing it wrong.

The incident happened during an aftercare group at a treatment center. The group assembled and started. The spotlight immediately glowed on one client, Jack, who had been sullen and snarly since he walked into the room. The therapist said he was aware Jack was disturbed. What was the matter? Jack said nothing was the matter. The therapist repeated his awareness and his question. Jack repeated his answer. The therapist paused. "He's lying! Confront him! Make him admit to the truth!" I urged silently. The rest of the group must have felt similar urges, because they all started hollering at Jack. The therapist sat back in his chair and held up his hand to quiet the group.

Jack said he had no intention of dealing with any problem because he didn't have one. The therapist said okay, that was fine, maybe Jack was right. But if he changed his mind and decided he had a problem and wanted to talk about it later, that would be fine, too. He said this with respect and without sarcasm, then proceeded to talk to someone else. "Well, we have just sold Jack down the stream," I thought. "Furthermore, he got one over on you."

17

An hour later, before the group ended, Jack said he guessed he did have a problem, and he hoped it didn't mean he was failing in his recovery program. He wasn't really aware of it before, he said, but he'd like to talk about it now, if that would be okay. It was.

The problem and its resolution aren't significant (except to Jack); the denial system was not colorful. What interested me, though, and what still does, is how the therapist dealt with it. Everything he did and said was contrary to what my first impulses told me to do. Since that time, I have encountered many people using denial. Some, like Jack, have stopped denying after a short while. Others have stopped it after longer periods. Some are still denying. Here are some suggestions that help me deal with other people's (and my own) denial.

1. Examine your motives. Do you really want to help the person, or are you trying to control or interfere? Are you angry, resentful, or afraid? Do you think you're "better" than this person is? Are you in touch with your feelings, beliefs, and Higher Power? Are you denying something? Do you have any need to deny what the other person is denying? Do you need or expect the other person to deny a thing for your own reasons? If you do, he or she may sense this and cooperate. If your heart is not right toward a person, he or she will sense this and you'll be rendered ineffective.

2. Stay healthy. Health begets health; illness is catchy. If at any time you decided you needed A.A., Al-Anon, or any of the Twelve Step programs, go to your meetings regularly and work your program. If you had a terminal, lifelong, incurable illness last year or ten years ago, you still have it. Treating it will minimize your need to use denial and the Twelve Steps will help you deal with other people.

3. Give healthy permissions. Allow yourself and others to think, feel, solve problems, be who they are, and be where they're at in their growth process. These permissions are empowering, energizing, and helpful. Because denial

short-circuits a person's thinking and emotional processes, giving these permissions may encourage the machinery to start working again. Giving people permission to be who they are — imperfect strugglers on a journey — may reduce their need to use denial. It's okay to have problems! It's okay to solve them, too.

A reverse permission I give people — especially young children who need to learn and people who have self-destructive tendencies is, "It's not okay to hurt yourself or others." This may be obvious to us but unclear to them.

4. Listen — if you want to. Let people know you're available if they want to talk. Talking helps people. They get things out of their heads and into the air. It's healing to be heard, really heard — it breeds acceptance. Remember, it helps to listen with your heart as well as your ears. What you're hearing might be another way of saying, "I'm scared," "I'm hurting," "I'm confused."

5. Talk about yourself, your emotions, and your experiences. Talking about your feelings is always one good way to work through them. It will help you. And, honestly reporting your emotions and experiences may help other people, too. It might encourage them to do the same; your victories may give them hope. Don't be pushy and don't preach. If you feel you must talk about another person instead of yourself, be gentle. People who are hurting respond well to gentleness. "Sounds like you're having problems," is more helpful than, "You're really screwed up." Better yet, find something good about that person — a quality, something he or she does that you like and appreciate — and offer that compliment. It could help that person more than you can know, and you will develop a valuable character trait.

What should you say to someone who asks you to support or agree to his or her denial? If someone asks you that important question, "Tell me it ain't so" — verbally or with an uncomfortable silence — here is one possible answer: "I cannot make that decision for you. You will have to think about it and decide for yourself." This should not only be an answer; it should be a deep attitude.

6. Offer information, literature, and referrals. That means *ask the person* if he or she wants you to leave the book, the pamphlet, or the article. If the answer is no, then don't. Remember, there's a difference between information and advice. Don't give or offer advice. It doesn't help and it just makes everyone mad. Even if you're asked, don't give advice. A good reply is, "What do you think you should do?" That's helpful, and no one gets angry.

7. Read the *Big Book (Alcoholics Anonymous,* published by A.A. World Services, available through Hazelden Educational Materials). It contains wisdom that has not yet been outdated.

8. Display empathy. That's a fancy word for putting yourself in the other person's place. It doesn't mean pity. It means remembering what it feels like to be facing a loss so painful you needed to deny it. If you cannot recall ever hurting or denying, and if you cannot empathize, see Number One above. If you still can't remember, perhaps you are not the person to be dealing with a hurting person. Empathy helps, and may greatly reduce the need for denial.

9. Avoid judgments. People have problems; the person is not the problem. Saying or believing a person is bad, inferior, hopeless, shameful, awful, or disgraceful will not help. Even if it's in our hearts, if we don't say it, it will not be heard. Experts believe fear, guilt, and shame are some of the biggest barriers people face to stop denying. If we add to a person's guilt and shame — if we say his or her worst fears are true — it won't help. It may increase the need to use denial.

10. Don't argue. It rarely helps a person stop denying. It diverts attention and wastes time and energy. You should not support or agree with denial, but neither should you attempt to pound reality into a person. Sometimes it helps to say, "Okay, maybe you're right." Then let it go. This takes the pressure off you and puts it on the other person in a positive, helpful way. Let people fight with themselves and decide if

they're right. Their battle with truth and reality is much tougher to win than a battle with you. And when that struggle is over, it will have accomplished something. This doesn't mean you can't feel angry towards a person using denial. You are entitled to your feelings, and you need to feel and sometimes communicate them. But shouting is not always the best way to do that.

11. Respect people. You don't have to respect unhealthy behaviors — respect the person. This includes believing they're okay (even if they have problems). They can think, and they can solve their problems. It means we allow them to do these things for themselves. Ask them what they think their problem is. Ask them how they would like to solve it. We don't have to "fix" them, make them better, control, or rescue them. We don't have to advise them or make their feelings go away. We don't have to and shouldn't get involved with their crises and consequences. Consequences are one way reality speaks loudly to those using denial. Quit bailing them out! You will do yourself and them a great kindness.

12. Respect yourself. Set boundaries — for your health and well-being. Don't do things for others that you truly don't want to do, that aren't good for you, or that aren't good for them. Don't let a person using denial do things to you that aren't good for you. This doesn't mean ultimatums or power plays (doing something to force another to do something or to "get even"). It means quietly figuring out what you need to do to take care of yourself, then doing it. Set limits.

13. Confront carefully. This is not a pamphlet on confrontation or intervention. Both are good tools, if used properly. Both can also be dangerous — to us and to the people we confront. Stripping a person of delusions is not a casual project. If the issue being denied is a serious one, the person may stop his or her denial upon confrontation. But remember — that person probably won't move serenely into acceptance. He or she may move into the second stage of the process — anger. I have witnessed violent and frightening acts when this

occurred. Be careful. John Powell explains why in, *Why Am I Afraid To Tell You Who I Am?:*

"The vocation of putting people straight, of tearing off their masks, of forcing them to face the repressed truth, is a highly dangerous and destructive calling," writes Powell. "He cannot live with some realization. In one way or another, he keeps his psychological pieces intact by some form of self-deception. . . . If the psychological pieces come unglued, who will pick them up and put poor Humpty Dumpty Human Being together again?"[9]

Seek professional help if you think you, or someone close to you, is having problems with extended denial or if you are considering a major confrontation or intervention.

14. Detach. The difficult behavior that helps so much. Don't take people personally, and don't take their problems, including denial, personally. We are not responsible for other adults — don't assume responsibility for them or their problems. Ultimately and absolutely, each person's denial is his problem. His acceptance process is his business. Mind your own business — yourself and your acceptance process. If we can't control others, which it seems we cannot, then we at least ought to try to gain control of ourselves. If you are having a hard time detaching from a person or a problem, maybe you want to consider Al-Anon. It helps.

15. Trust yourself, the acceptance process, and your Higher Power. There are no absolute rules for dealing with denial or for dealing with people. Each situation and person is unique. But you can think, and you can figure out how to handle situations. If you want to help someone, ask your Higher Power to use you and to show you what to do. Strive for gentleness, clear thinking, and love in your encounters with people. Forget perfection.

---

[9] Powell, John, S.J., *Why Am I Afraid To Tell You Who I Am?* (Allen, Texas: Argus Communication, 1969), pp. 116-117. Available through Hazelden Educational Materials, Order No. 6670

And you don't always have to do something. People "get it together" by falling apart — and the process often begins with denial. That's how God works with us. Let go and let Him!